Pebble® Plus

Healthy Teeth

Flossing Teeth

by Mari Schuh

Consulting Editor:
Gail Saunders-Smith, PhD

Consultant:
Lori Gagliardi CDA, RDA, RDH, Ed.D

Capstone press®

Mankato, Minnesota

Pebble Plus is published by Capstone Press,
151 Good Counsel Drive, P.O. Box 669, Mankato, Minnesota 56002.
www.capstonepress.com

1 2 3 4 5 6 13 12 11 10 09 08

Library of Congress Cataloging-in-Publication Data
Schuh, Mari C., 1975–
    Flossing teeth/by Mari Schuh.
    p. cm. — (Pebble plus. Healthy teeth)
    Summary: "Simple text, photographs, and diagrams present information about flossing teeth properly"—
Provided by publisher.
    Includes bibliographical references and index.
    ISBN-13: 978-1-4296-1241-8 (hardcover)
    ISBN-10: 1-4296-1241-X (hardcover)
    ISBN-13: 978-1-4296-1787-1 (softcover)
    ISBN-10: 1-4296-1787-X (softcover)
    1. Teeth — Care and hygiene — Juvenile literature. I. Title. II. Series.
RK63.S39 2008
617.6'01 — dc22   2007027118

Editorial Credits
Sarah L. Schuette, editor; Veronica Bianchini, designer and illustrator

Photo Credits
Capstone Press/Karon Dubke, all

The author dedicates this book to her friend, Liz Odom of Fairmont, Minnesota, whose path to self-care
began with flossing her teeth.

Note to Parents and Teachers

The Healthy Teeth set supports national science standards related to personal health.
This book describes and illustrates flossing teeth. The images support early readers in
understanding the text. The repetition of words and phrases helps early readers learn
new words. This book also introduces early readers to subject-specific vocabulary words,
which are defined in the Glossary section. Early readers may need assistance to read
some words and to use the Table of Contents, Glossary, Read More, Internet Sites, and
Index sections of the book.

Table of Contents

Why Floss?

Anna flosses her teeth once every day. Flossing cleans where her toothbrush can't reach.

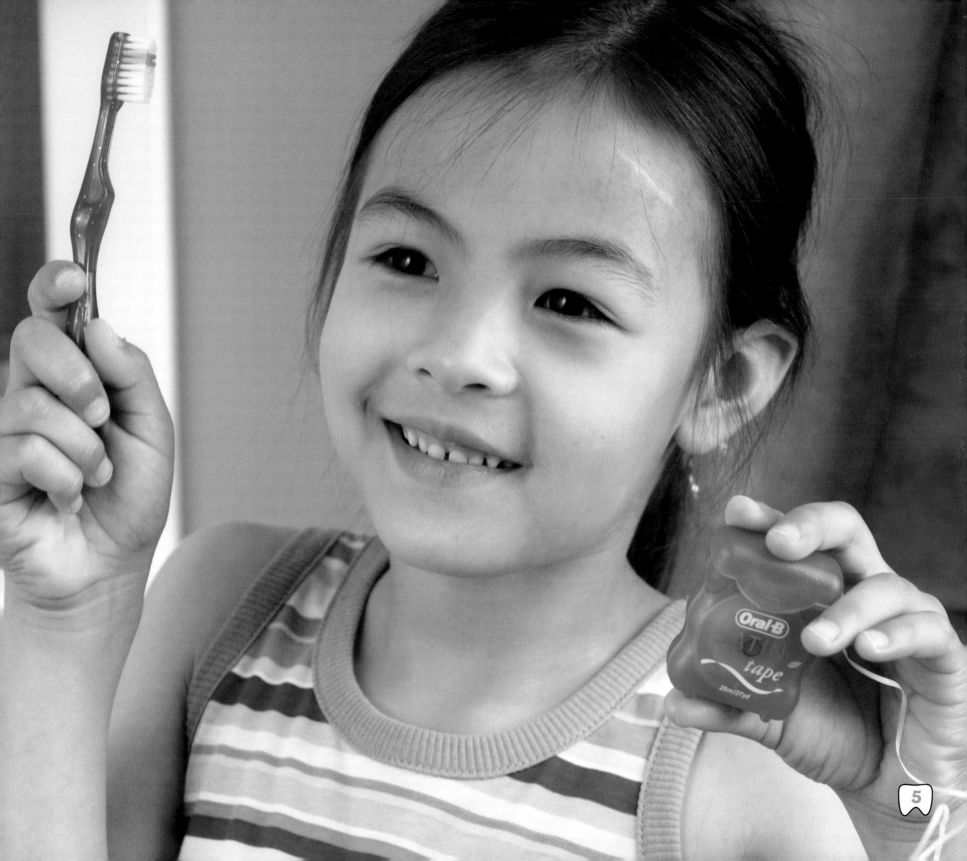

Flossing gets rid of
food and plaque stuck
in your teeth.
Plaque causes cavities.

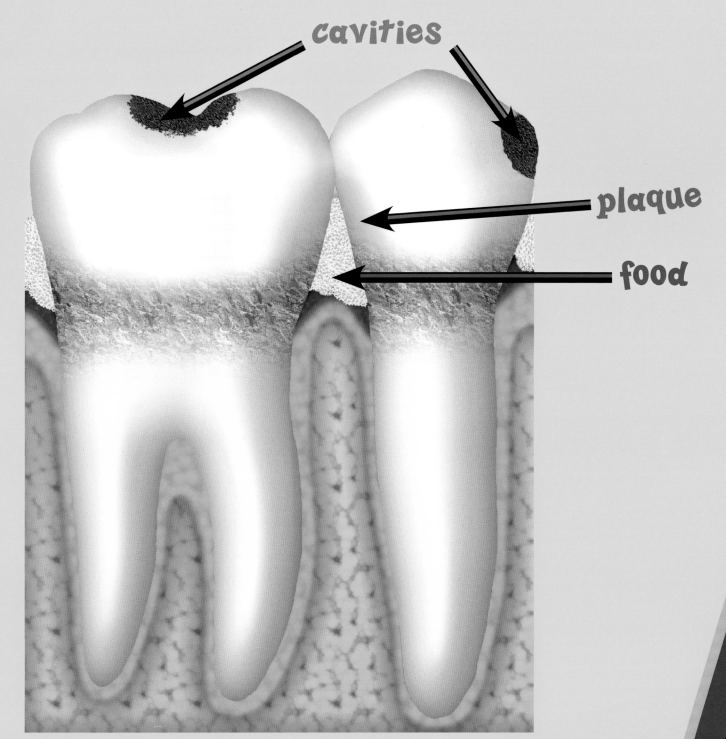

cavities

plaque

food

Dental floss is
a thin piece of string.
Floss comes in many flavors
and colors.

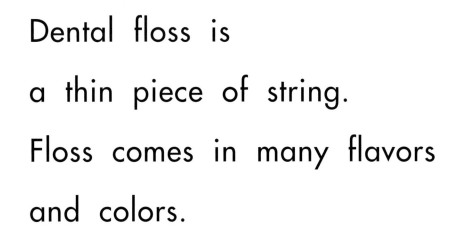

Flossing

Anna pulls out a piece
of floss about the length
of her arm.
She wraps it loosely around
her fingers.

Anna gently slides
the minty floss
between two teeth.
She moves it up and down
and back and forth.

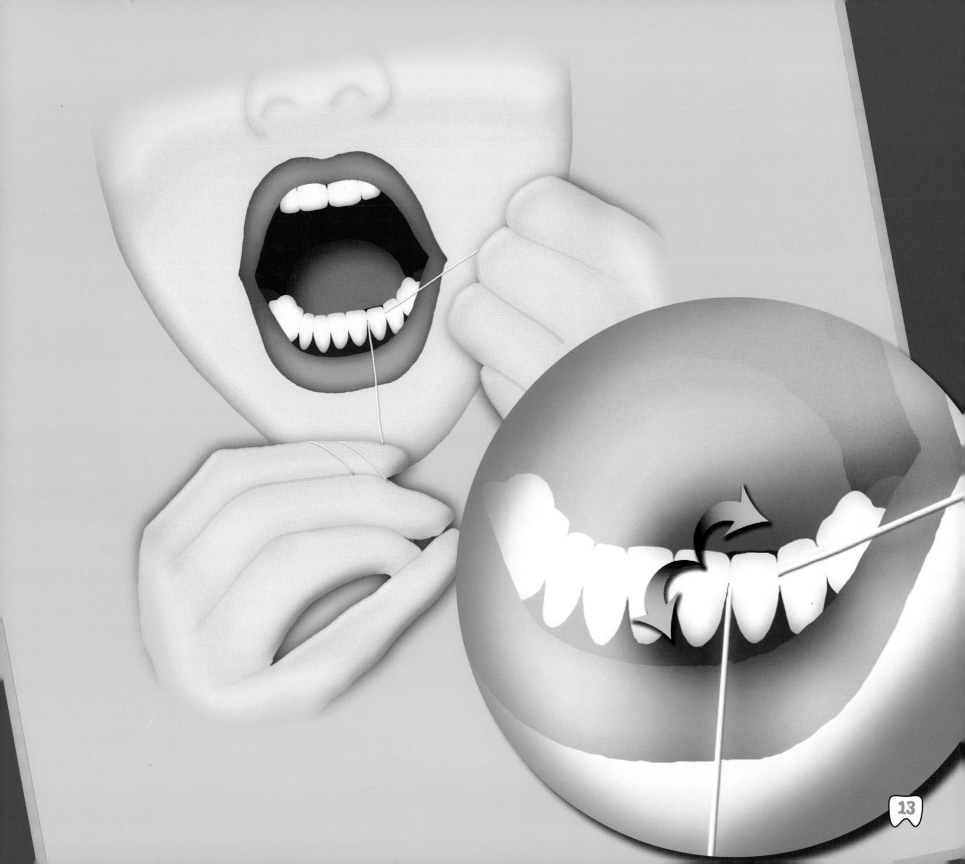

Anna flosses in a pattern.
She makes sure to get
between all her teeth.
Anna uses a new section
of floss for each tooth.

Anna tries a flossing tool.
It makes flossing
easier for her.

Anna rinses her mouth
after flossing.
She throws away
the used floss.
She's done!

Healthy Teeth

Flossing your teeth
will help you have
a healthy smile too!

Glossary

cavity — a decayed part or hole in a tooth

gum — the firm skin around the base of a tooth

length — the distance from one end of something to the other

pattern — a repeated set of actions; flossing in the same pattern helps you remember to get between all of your teeth every time you floss.

plaque — a sticky coating that forms on your teeth from food, bacteria, and saliva in your mouth

tooth — one of the white, bony parts of your mouth that you use for biting and chewing food

Read More

Curry, Don. L. *Take Care of Your Teeth.* Rookie Read-About Health. New York: Children's Press, 2005.

DeGezelle, Terri. *Taking Care of My Teeth.* Pebble Plus: Keeping Healthy. Mankato, Minn.: Capstone Press, 2006.

Llewellyn, Claire. *Your Teeth.* Look After Yourself. North Mankato, Minn.: Sea to Sea Publishing, 2007.

Internet Sites

FactHound offers a safe, fun way to find Internet sites related to this book. All of the sites on FactHound have been researched by our staff.

Here's how:

1. Visit *www.facthound.com*

2. Choose your grade level.

3. Type in this book ID **142961241X** for age-appropriate sites. You may also browse subjects by clicking on letters, or by clicking on pictures and words.

4. Click on the **Fetch It** button.

FactHound will fetch the best sites for you!

Index

Word Count: 142
Grade: 1
Early-Intervention Level: 18